I0606308

# MOUNTAIN BIKING

OUTDOOR ADVENTURES and SPORTS

Michael De Medeiros

AV2
www.openlightbox.com

**Step 1**
Go to **www.openlightbox.com**

**Step 2**
Enter this unique code
**TGYNIX9KU**

**Step 3**
Explore your interactive eBook!

**AV2 is optimized for use on any device**

# Your interactive eBook comes with...

**Contents**
Browse a live contents page to easily navigate through resources

**Audio**
Listen to sections of the book read aloud

**Videos**
Watch informative video clips

**Weblinks**
Gain additional information for research

**Slideshows**
View images and captions

**Try This!**
Complete activities and hands-on experiments

**Key Words**
Study vocabulary, and complete a matching word activity

**Quizzes**
Test your knowledge

**Share**
Share titles within your Learning Management System (LMS) or Library Circulation System

**Citation**
Create bibliographical references following the Chicago Manual of Style

**This title is part of our AV2 digital subscription**

**1-Year K–5 Subscription**
**ISBN** 978-1-7911-3320-7

Access hundreds of AV2 titles with our digital subscription.
Sign up for a FREE trial at **www.openlightbox.com/trial**

OUTDOOR ADVENTURES and SPORTS

# MOUNTAIN BIKING

CONTENTS

# All About Mountain Biking

Since the first bicycle was built, people have been riding bikes in the mountains. However, it was not until the 1970s that modern mountain biking emerged as a sport. Many people believe the sport originally developed in California.

In the late 1960s, mountain bikers rode klunker bikes. Klunker bikes were old **cruiser** bikes with added homemade parts, fat tires, and better brakes. Cyclists would race down short, steep hills, dirt roads, and mountain trails. They timed themselves to see who could race downhill the fastest.

Mountain biking has become more than a fun activity for people of all ages. It is a sport practiced around the world. There are national competitions in almost every country and several international competitions, such as the Olympic Games.

Mountain biking continues to become more popular. Each year, many people learn how to mountain bike. They consider it a fun way to keep fit and a challenging sport in which to compete.

# Changes Throughout the Years

| PAST | PRESENT |
|---|---|
| Riders moved bicycles by pushing the ground with their feet. | Mountain bikes and other modern bikes have pedals. |
| Bicycles had only one gear. | Most mountain bikes have between 21 and 27 gears, although some have fewer and others have more. |
| Women's bikes had a low top bar so that women could wear skirts while cycling. | Both men and women can ride bikes with high top bars and wear shorts or pants. |
| People did not use safety gear while cycling. | Most people wear a helmet and reflectors while cycling. |

# Getting Started

Mountain biking can be dangerous. It is important to have the proper equipment to enjoy a safe ride. Having the right bike to ride is an important part of mountain biking.

A mountain bike is different from a road bike. It must work well on bumpy, wet mountain trails. A mountain bike has a strong frame that will not bend or break from rough use. The fatter tires on a mountain bike grip the ground better than thin road tires. Mountain bikes also have more gears, which are used to adjust to the ever-changing terrain, or ground.

Mountain bikes are lower to the ground than road bikes so that riders are closer to the trail. This keeps riders more stable and makes them less likely to fall. A mountain bike's handlebars are raised higher than those of a road bike. This makes it easier to pull up on the handlebars and lift the front end of the bike over rocks, tree roots, or other objects on a trail.

**1** A helmet protects the rider's head if he or she falls off the bike.

**2** Special mountain biking gloves are important. Gloves protect hands from being scratched while riding or during a fall. Gloves also give the rider a better grip on the handlebars.

**3** Sunglasses keep sunlight, dirt, bugs, and wind from getting in the rider's eyes.

Mountain bikers should wear tight clothing to prevent fabric from rubbing against their skin as they ride.

**4** A trail repair kit can help fix tires, brakes, and other parts that might become damaged during a ride. A mini air pump for easy tire **inflation** should be part of every trail repair kit.

**5** Reflectors or reflective clothing ensure that riders can be seen by other cyclists or people. This helps riders avoid accidents on the trail.

**6** In warm weather, padded mountain bike shorts make the ride more comfortable. In cold and wet weather, riders should wear a waterproof jacket, winter tights, boots, and winter gloves.

# Mountain Biking Basics

Before beginning a mountain biking trip, riders should know basic biking moves and techniques. Knowing these basics will help riders stay safe and enjoy their trip.

First, it is necessary to know how to **mount** a mountain bike. To mount a bike, make sure that the seat, or saddle, is set at the right height. After sitting on the saddle, the rider should be able to reach the lowest pedal with only a slight bend in the knee. If the leg does not reach the pedal, the saddle is too high. If the leg is bent, the saddle is too low.

After adjusting the saddle, riders should check the gears. Higher gears make it easier to pedal. They are used for riding uphill. Lower gears make it harder to pedal. They are used for flat or downhill terrain.

Mountain bikers should shift gears before beginning a downhill or uphill ride. It is safest to change gears while on flat ground. This also helps reduce wear on the gears.

When riders reach a muddy, sandy, or wet patch of land, it is important to shift the bike into a higher gear. It is more difficult to pedal over muddy, sandy, or wet ground. Using a higher gear allows the rider to keep moving instead of becoming stuck. Mountain bikers should also know how to lean their weight toward the back end of the bike. This will help the front wheel slide across the ground.

Mountain bikers should not grip the handlebars too tightly. This will make the upper body tense and tire the rider faster. Riders should place their thumbs below the handlebars, keep their elbows bent, and ensure their shoulders are loose.

Pack an old cotton sock or spare piece of cloth. It will make for a nice grease rag if your bike chain falls off, and you need to clean your hands after fixing it.

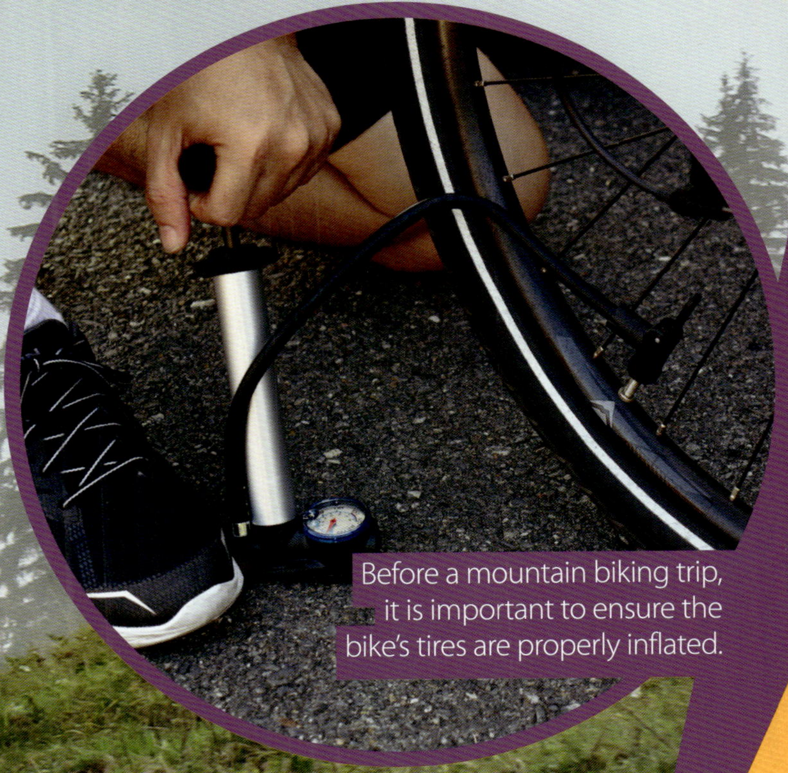

Before a mountain biking trip, it is important to ensure the bike's tires are properly inflated.

# Mountain Biking Levels

Mountain biking can be easy or challenging, depending on the rider's experience and the difficulty of the trail. Riders can help to ensure a safe and fun mountain biking experience by being prepared with the proper equipment and training.

Planning a **route** based on how far mountain bikers want to ride is important. Most people enjoy afternoon, day, or weekend trips. After deciding the distance of a ride, it is important to plan breaks. Most riders plan their stops around the more difficult parts of their route. If the path is known to have wet or muddy areas, riders often stop right before those points. These stops allow riders to rest before tackling a challenging part of the trail.

Most mountain bike racing paths have sections for beginners and others for more experienced riders. Experienced riders often prefer specialized paths because they are more challenging. Specialized paths test many mountain biking skills, such as steering, speed, handling, and uphill and downhill riding.

Learning to ride through mud and water takes practice. For beginning riders, it is best to avoid these conditions if possible.

Some mountain bike tires are made from the same material used in bulletproof vests. These are less likely to puncture on rough terrain.

## Average Biking Distances for Experienced Riders

**AFTERNOON**
10 to 15 miles (16 to 24 kilometers)

**FULL-DAY WITH STOPS**
20 to 25 miles (32 to 40 km)

**FULL-DAY, OFF-ROAD TRIP**
50 miles (80 km)

# Staying Safe

Mountain biking can be fun and exciting, but it is an **extreme sport**. Riders need to know how to avoid hazards on trails and how they can best protect themselves from injury.

When riders travel over rough terrain, they may be thrown from the bike. Broken bones, scrapes, and bruises are all risks of a challenging ride. All riders should carry a basic first aid kit that has bandages, moist towelettes, and scissors.

Riders should know their abilities and keep to paths that are not too difficult for their skill level. It is important to know where the path leads and how long it will take to ride from beginning to end. This will ensure that riders do not become lost and are not out at night when the trail is hard to see. Proper planning will help riders finish their routes.

Like any outdoor activity, mountain biking is affected by the weather. It is more difficult to bike in wet, muddy conditions. Riders should check local weather reports before riding. Try to plan trips on warm, sunny days.

**Important Mountain Biking Supplies**

Extra Clothing

Water

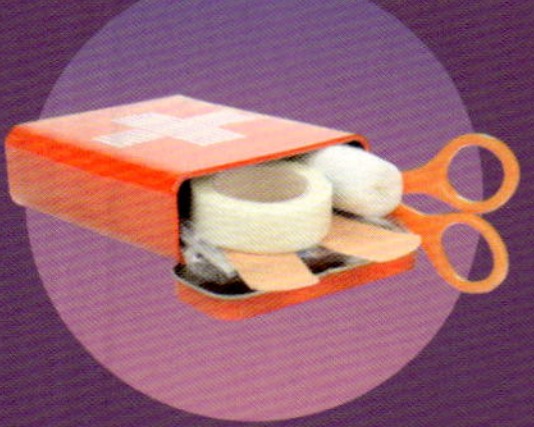

First Aid Kit

# #2 Mountain Biking Tip

Plan your route carefully before taking a bike ride. Carrying a compass and a map can help show the way home if you become lost. Make sure to tell another person where you are going and when you plan to return.

When braking, riders should be sure to pull both the front and back brakes at the same time. Pulling only the front brake may cause the bike to tip forward, throwing the rider over the handlebars.

# Explore the Outdoors

There are many other ways to explore the outdoors in the mountains. These activities include mountain climbing, snowboarding, bicycle motocross racing, and cycling.

## Mountain Climbing

Mountain climbing, which is sometimes called mountaineering, is the act of climbing mountains, rocks, and ice. Climbing requires special equipment, such as ropes and harnesses, to keep climbers safe. People climb for sport, research, or recreation.

## Snowboarding

Snowboarding is similar to skiing. However, snowboarders use one wide board instead of two long, thin skis. Snowboarders ride down snow-covered runs on ski hills. Like surfing and skateboarding, snowboarding became common in the United States in the 1980s. It was accepted into the Olympics in 1998 as a competitive sport.

## Bicycle Motocross Racing

Bicycle motocross, or BMX, racing is a combination of mountain biking and cycling. It is an extreme sport. Racers wear helmets that cover their faces. They also wear padding that acts as a suit of protective armor. BMX racing often takes place on sand tracks that have large hills, ramps, and other obstacles.

## Cycling

Cycling is the oldest sport that uses a bicycle. Cyclists take part in races on **closed courses** around the world. Cycling can be a team or single-person sport. Cyclists can reach speeds of more than 70 miles (113 km) per hour. The Tour de France is the biggest international cycling competition. There are also cycling competitions in the Olympics.

# Mountain Biking Around the World

Mountain biking can be done in almost every country in the world. Some riders like to plan routes in different cities, traveling many miles to view unique scenery and terrain. The following mountain biking areas are thought to be among the best in the world.

## 1 Seven Summits Trail, Canada

One of the most adventurous mountain biking areas in the world, Seven Summits has more than 19 miles (30 km) of trails.

## 2 Moab, United States

Canyon country in Moab, Utah, has areas of desert and mountain terrain, sandstone arches, and large canyons.

## 3 Falun, Sweden

Although not as hilly as some areas, Falun includes long-distance trails and challenging terrain, such as rocks and exposed tree roots.

## 4 Swiss Alps, Switzerland

This area is known for its challenging trails and spectacular views. A tour of the Swiss Alps is considered by many riders to be an ideal mountain bike trip.

# Join the Club

The International Mountain Bicycling Association (IMBA) is one of the best-known mountain biking associations in the world. The association was formed in 1988. Five riding clubs in California joined together to form the IMBA. The clubs were the Off-Road Bicyclists Association, Bicycle Trails Council Marin, Bicycle Trails Council East Bay, Responsible Organized Mountain Pedalers, and Sacramento Rough Riders.

The IMBA works to create and preserve mountain biking trails all over the world. It encourages volunteer trail work and **low-impact** riding. The IMBA also works to keep trails open to riders. It has about 35,000 members around the world.

Competitive international mountain biking began at the 1990 Mountain Bike World Championships. Since then, the sport has grown quickly and gained many fans. Mountain biking became an Olympic competition during the 1996 Atlanta Olympic Games. At the Olympics, riders compete in a cross-country mountain biking event. They must cross 25 to 30 miles (40 to 50 km) of rugged terrain, with hills, rocks, trees, and streams. The event takes athletes 80 to 100 minutes to finish.

Riding clubs encourage mountain bikers to ride together in a group. This can be a way for beginners to learn from more experienced riders.

Downhill racing is a popular off-road competition for mountain bikers.

# Healthy Habits

A balanced diet is the first step toward a healthy and active lifestyle. Meals that include the four food groups give mountain bikers the minerals and energy they need to enjoy a full day of riding. The four food groups are dairy, grains, vegetables and fruits, and protein.

While riding, it is important to stay hydrated. This means riders must drink water often. Not all water is safe to drink. Some sources of water may carry **bacteria** that can cause illness. Mountain bikers should bring a supply of water. It is not safe to drink from lakes or streams.

Mountain bikers need to maintain their physical fitness. They must have well-developed leg muscles to pedal the bike. Fit arms are needed to steer. A strong back helps riders keep their balance on bumpy trails.

Mountain biking takes riders outside and into the fresh air. It challenges riders physically and increases energy levels.

Before taking mountain biking trips, there are a few basic warmup exercises that riders should perform. They are the knee bend, side stretch, spine reflex, and thigh stretch. These basic stretching exercises loosen muscles, which helps prevent injuries.

When biking in the Sun for more than 30 minutes, it is important to use sunscreen.

## Stretches

Try practicing these stretches before biking to improve flexibility and prevent injury. Be sure to hold each stretch for 15 seconds.

**KNEE BEND**
Stand with one hand holding onto a chair for balance. Bend the right leg, and grasp the foot with the right hand. Pull the foot towards the buttocks until a stretch is felt. Repeat with the left leg.

**SIDE STRETCH**
Point your left arm toward the ceiling. Place your right hand on your hip. Bend your body to the right. Repeat with your other arm while bending to the left.

**SPINE REFLEX**
Lean back without lying down to balance the weight of your legs.

**THIGH STRETCH**
Stand with one leg in front of the other. Lean your upper body forward on the front leg. Repeat with the other leg in front.

# Quiz

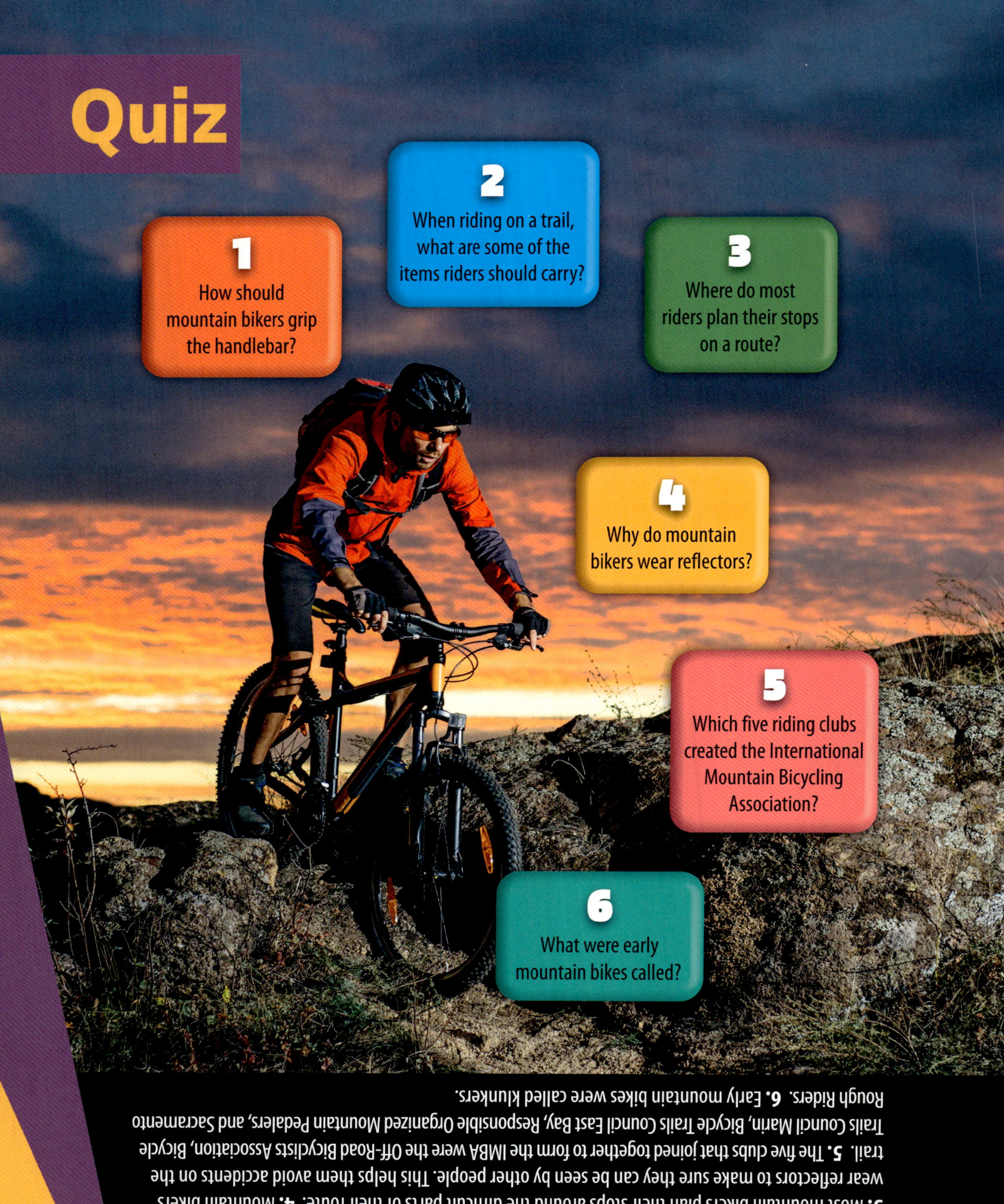

**1**
How should mountain bikers grip the handlebar?

**2**
When riding on a trail, what are some of the items riders should carry?

**3**
Where do most riders plan their stops on a route?

**4**
Why do mountain bikers wear reflectors?

**5**
Which five riding clubs created the International Mountain Bicycling Association?

**6**
What were early mountain bikes called?

**Answers**

**1.** They should have their thumbs below the handlebars, keep their elbows bent, and ensure their shoulders are loose. **2.** Riders should carry extra clothing, water, a first aid kit, and a trail repair kit. **3.** Most mountain bikers plan their stops around the difficult parts of their route. **4.** Mountain bikers wear reflectors to make sure they can be seen by other people. This helps them avoid accidents on the trail. **5.** The five clubs that joined together to form the IMBA were the Off-Road Bicyclists Association, Bicycle Trails Council Marin, Bicycle Trails Council East Bay, Responsible Organized Mountain Pedalers, and Sacramento Rough Riders. **6.** Early mountain bikes were called klunkers.

# Key Words

**bacteria:** organisms that spread disease
**closed courses:** courses for competition that only those competing can enter
**cruiser:** a balloon-tired bike with a heavy-duty frame that was popular in the United States from the 1930s to 1970s
**extreme sport:** difficult or dangerous athletic activity
**inflation:** the amount of air in a tire
**low-impact:** not damaging to the environment
**mount:** the act of getting into a seated position on a mountain bike
**route:** the path or trail a mountain biker rides

# Index

# Get the best of both worlds.

AV2 bridges the gap between print and digital.

The expandable resources toolbar enables quick access to content including **videos**, **audio**, **activities**, **weblinks**, **slideshows**, **quizzes**, and **key words**.

**Animated videos** make static images come alive.

Resource icons on each page help readers to further **explore key concepts**.

Published by Lightbox Learning Inc.
276 5th Avenue, Suite 704 #917
New York, NY 10001
Website: www.openlightbox.com



Library of Congress Cataloging-in-Publication Data

Names: De Medeiros, Michael, author.
Title: Mountain biking / Michael De Medeiros.
Description: New York, NY : Lightbox Learning Inc., 2023. | Series: Outdoor adventures and sports | Includes index. | Audience: Grades 4-6
Identifiers: LCCN 2022023898 (print) | LCCN 2022023899 (ebook) | ISBN 9781791147488 (library binding) | ISBN 9781791147495 (paperback) | ISBN 9781791147501
Subjects: LCSH: Mountain biking--Juvenile literature.
Classification: LCC GV1056 .D393 2023 (print) | LCC GV1056 (ebook) | DDC 796.63--dc23/eng/20220526
LC record available at https://lccn.loc.gov/2022023898
LC ebook record available at https://lccn.loc.gov/2022023899

Printed in Guangzhou, China
1 2 3 4 5 6 7 8 9 0 26 25 24 23 22

062022
101121

**Project Coordinator** Priyanka Das
**Designer** Terry Paulhus

**Photo Credits**
Every reasonable effort has been made to trace ownership and to obtain permission to reprint copyright material. The publisher would be pleased to have any errors or omissions brought to its attention so that they may be corrected in subsequent printings. The publisher acknowledges Getty Images and Shutterstock as its primary image suppliers for this title.